THE STAIRCASE AT THE HEARTS DELIGHT

ANNA KATHARINE GREENE

[ZHINGOORA BOOKS]

This edition is published by
Zhingoora Books.

AS TOLD BY MR. GRYCE.

"In the spring of 1840, the attention of the New York police was attracted by the many cases of well-known men found drowned in the various waters surrounding the lower portion of our great city. Among these may be mentioned the name of Elwood Henderson, the noted tea merchant, whose remains were washed ashore at Redhook Point; and of Christopher Bigelow, who was picked up off Governor's Island after having been in the water for five days, and of another well-known millionaire whose name I cannot now recall, but who, I remember, was seen to walk towards the East River one March evening, and was not met with again till the 5th of April, when his body floated into one of the docks near Peck Slip.

"As it seemed highly improbable that there should have been a concerted action among so many wealthy and distinguished men to end their lives within a few weeks of each other, and all by the same method of drowning, we soon became suspicious that a more serious verdict than that of suicide should have been rendered in the case of Henderson, Bigelow and the other gentleman I have mentioned. Yet one fact, common to all these cases, pointed so conclusively to deliberate intention on the part of the sufferers that we hesitated to take action.

"This was, that upon the body of each of the above-mentioned persons there were found, not only valuables in the shape of money and jewelry, but papers and memoranda of a nature calculated to fix the identity of the drowned man, in case the water should rob him of his personal characteristics. Consequently, we could not ascribe these deaths to a desire for plunder on the part of some unknown person.

"I was a young man in those days, and full of ambition. So, though I said nothing, I did not let this matter drop when the others did, but kept my mind persistently upon it and waited, with odd results as you will hear, for another victim to be reported at police headquarters.

"Meantime I sought to discover some bond or connection between the several men who had been found drowned, which would serve to explain their similar fate. But all my efforts in this direction were fruitless. There was no bond between them, and the matter remained for a while an unsolved mystery.

"Suddenly one morning a clew was placed, not in my hands, but in those of a superior official who at that time exerted a great influence over the whole force. He was sitting in his private room, when there was ushered into his presence a young man of a dissipated but not unprepossessing appearance, who, after a pause of marked embarrassment, entered upon the following story:

"I don't know whether or no, I should offer an excuse for the communication I am about to make; but the matter I have to relate is simply this: Being hard up last night (for though a rich man's son I often lack money), I went to a certain pawn-shop in the Bowery where I had been told I could raise money on my prospects. This place—you may see it sometime, so I will not enlarge upon it—did not strike me favorably; but, being very anxious for a certain definite sum of money, I wrote my name in a book which was brought to me from some unknown quarter, and proceeded to follow the young woman who attended me into what she was pleased to call her good master's private office. He may have been a good master, but he was anything but a good man, In short, sir, when he found out who I was, and how much I needed money, he suggested that I should make an appointment with my father at a place he called Judah's in Grand Street, where, said he, 'your little affair will be arranged, and you made a rich man within thirty days. That is,' he slyly added, 'unless your father has already made a will, disinheriting you.'

"I was shocked, sir, shocked beyond all my powers of concealment, not so much at his words, which I hardly understood, as at his looks, which had a world of evil suggestion in them; so I raised my fist and would have knocked him down, only that I found two young fellows at my elbows, who held me quiet for five minutes, while the old fellow talked to me. He asked me if I came to him on a fool's errand or really to get money; and when I admitted that I had cherished hopes of obtaining a clear two thousand dollars from him, he coolly replied that he knew of but one way in which I could hope to get such an amount, and that if I was too squeamish to adopt it, I had made a mistake in coming to his shop, which was no missionary institution, etc., etc. Not wishing to irritate him, for there was menace in his eye, I asked, with a certain weak show of being sorry for my former heat, whereabouts in Grand Street I should find this Judah. The retort was quick, 'Judah is not his name,' said he, 'and Grand Street is not where you are to go to find him. I threw out a bait to see if you would snap at it, but I find you timid, and therefore advise you to drop the matter entirely.' I was quite willing to do so, and answered him to this effect; whereupon, with a side glance I did not understand but which made me more or less uneasy in regard to his intentions towards me, he motioned to the men who held my arms to let go their hold, which they at once did.

"'We have your signature,' growled the old man as I went out. 'If you peach on us or trouble us in any way we will show it to your father and that will put an end to all your hopes of future fortune.' Then raising his voice he shouted to the girl in the outer office, 'Let the young man see what he has signed.' She smiled and again brought forward the book in which I had so recklessly placed my name, and there at the top of the page I read these words: 'For moneys received, I agree to notify Levi Solomon, within the month, of the death of my father, that he may recover from me, without loss of time, the sum of ten thousand dollars from the amount I am bound to receive as my father's heir.' The sight of these lines knocked me hollow. But I am less of a coward morally than physically, and I determined to acquaint my father at once with what I had done, and get his advice as to whether or not I should inform the police of my adventure. He heard me with more consideration than I expected, but insisted that I should immediately make known to you my experience in this Bowery pawnbroker's shop.

"The officer, highly interested, took down the young man's statement in writing, and, after getting a more accurate description of the Jew's house, allowed his visitor to go.

"Fortunately for me I was in the building at the time, and was able to respond when a man was called up to investigate this matter. Thinking that I saw a connection between it and the various mysterious deaths of which I have previously spoken, I entered into the affair with much spirit. But, wishing to be sure that my possibly unwarranted conclusions were correct, I took pains to inquire, before proceeding upon my errand, into the character of the heirs who had inherited the property of Elwood Henderson and Christopher Bigelow, and found that in each case there was one among the rest who was well known for his profligacy and reckless expenditure. It was a significant discovery, and increased, if possible, my interest in running down this nefarious trafficker in the lives of wealthy men.

"Knowing that I could hope for no success in my character of detective, I made an arrangement with the father of the young gentleman before alluded to, by which I was to enter the pawn-shop as an emissary of the latter. I accordingly appeared there, one dull November afternoon, in the garb of a certain western sporting man, who, for a consideration, allowed me the temporary use of his name and credentials.

"Entering beneath the three golden balls, with, the swagger and general air of ownership I thought most likely to impose upon the self-satisfied female who presided over the desk, I asked to see her boss.

"'On your own business?' she queried, glancing with suspicion at my short coat, which was rather more showy than elegant.

"'No,' I returned, 'not on my own business, but on that of a young gent——'

"'Anyone whose name is written here?' she interposed, reaching towards me the famous book, over the top of which, however, she was careful to lay her arm.

"I glanced down the page she had opened and instantly detected that of the young gentleman on whose behalf I was supposed to be there, and nodded 'Yes,' with all the assurance of which I was capable.

"'Very well, then,' said she, 'come!' and she ushered me without much ado into a den of discomfort where sat a man, with a great beard and such heavy overhanging eyebrows that I could hardly detect the twinkle of his eyes, keen and incisive as they were.

"Smiling upon him, but not in the same way I had upon the girl, I glanced behind me at the open door, and above me at the partitions, which failed to reach the ceiling. Then I shook my head and drew a step nearer.

"'I have come,' I insinuatingly whispered, 'on behalf of a certain party who left this place in a huff a day or so ago, but who since then has had time to think the matter over, and has sent me with an apology which he hopes'—here I put on a diabolical smile, copied, I declare to you, from the one I saw at that moment on his own lips—'you will accept.'

"The old wretch regarded me for full two minutes in a way to unmask me had I possessed less confidence in my disguise and in my ability to support it.

"'And what is this young gentleman's name?' he finally asked.

"For reply, I handed him a slip of paper. He took it and read the few lines written on it, after which he began to rub his palms together with a snaky unction eminently in keeping with the stray glints of light that now and then found their way through his' bushy eyebrows.

"'And so the young gentleman had not the courage to come again himself?' he softly suggested, with just the suspicion of an ironical laugh. 'Thought, perhaps, I would exact too much commission; or make him pay too roundly for his impertinent assurance.'

"I shrugged my shoulders, but vouchsafed no immediate reply, and he saw that he had to open the business himself. He did it warily and with many an incisive question which would have tripped me up if I had not been very much on my guard; but it all ended, as such matters usually do, in mutual understanding, and a promise that if the young gentleman was willing to sign a certain paper, which, by the way, was not shown me, he would in exchange give him an address which, if made proper use of, would lead to my patron finding himself an independent man within a very few days.

"As this address was the thing above all others which I most desired, I professed myself satisfied with the arrangement, and proceeded to hunt up my patron, as he was called. Informing him of the result of my visit, I asked if his interest in ferreting out these criminals was strong enough to lead him to sign the vile document which the Jew would probably have in readiness for him on the morrow; and being told it was, we separated for that day, with the understanding that we were to meet the next morning at the spot chosen by the Jew for the completion of his nefarious bargain.

"Being certain that I was being followed in all my movements by the agents of this adept in villainy, I took care, upon leaving Mr. L———, to repair to the hotel of the sporting man I was personifying. Making myself square with the proprietor, I took up my quarters in the room of my sporting friend, and, the better to deceive any spy who might be lurking about, I received his letters and sent out his telegrams, which, if they did not create confusion in the affairs of 'The Plunger,' must at least have occasioned him no little work the next day.

"Promptly at ten o'clock on the following morning I met my patron at the place of rendezvous appointed by the old Jew; and when I tell you that this was no other than the old cemetery of which a portion is still to be seen off Chatham Square, you will understand the uncanny nature of this whole adventure, and the lurking sense there was in it of brooding death and horror. The scene, which in these days is disturbed by elevated railroad trains and the flapping of long lines of parti-colored clothes strung high up across the quiet tombstones, was at that time one of peaceful rest, in the midst of a quarter devoted to everything for which that rest is the fitting and desirable end; and as we paused among the mossy stones, we found it hard to realize that in a few minutes there would be standing beside us the concentrated essence of all that was evil and despicable in human nature.

"He arrived with a smile on his countenance that completed his ugliness, and would have frightened any honest man from his side at once. Merely glancing my way, he shuffled up to my companion, and leading him aside, drew out a paper which he laid on a flat tombstone with a gesture significant of his desire that the other should affix to it the required signature.

"Meantime I stood guard, and while attempting to whistle a light air, was carelessly taking in the surroundings, and conjecturing, as best I might, the reasons which had induced the old ghoul to make use of this spot for his diabolical business, and had about decided that it was because he was a ghoul, and thus felt at home among the symbols of mortality, when I caught sight of two or three young fellows, who were lounging on the other side of the fence.

"These were so evidently accomplices that I wondered if the two sly boys I had engaged to stand by me through this affair had spotted them, and would know enough to follow them back to their haunts.

"A few minutes later, the old rascal came sneaking towards me, with a gleam of satisfaction in his half-closed eyes.

"'You are not wanted any longer,' he grunted. 'The young gentleman told me to say that he could look out for himself now.'

"'The young gentleman had better pay me the round fifty he promised me,' I grumbled in return, with that sudden change from indifference to menace which I thought best calculated to further my plans; and shouldering the miserable wretch aside, I stepped up to my companion, who was still lingering in a state of hesitation among the gravestones.

"'Quick! Tell me the number and street which he has given you! 'I whispered, in a tone strangely in contrast with the angry and reproachful air I had assumed.

"He was about to answer, when the old fellow came sidling up behind us. Instantly the young man before me rose to the occasion, and putting on an air of conciliation said in a soothing tone:

"'There, there, don't bluster. Do one thing more for me, and I will add another fifty to those I promised you. Conjure up an anonymous letter—you know how—and send it to my father, saying that if he wants to know where his son loses his hundreds, he must go to the place on the dock, opposite 5 South Street, some night shortly after nine. It would not work with most men, but it will with my father, and when he has been in and out of that place, and I succeed to the fortune he will leave me, then I will remember you, and——'

"'Say, too,' a sinister voice here added in my ear, 'that if he wishes to effect an entrance into the gambling den which his son haunts, he must take the precaution of tying a bit of blue ribbon in his button-hole. It is a signal meaning business, and must not be forgotten,' chuckled the old fellow, evidently deceived at last into thinking I was really one of his own kind.

"I answered by a wink, and taking care to attempt no further communication with my patron, I left the two, as soon as possible, and went back to the hotel, where I dropped 'the sport,' and assumed a character and dress which enabled me to make my way undetected to the house of my young patron, where for two days I lay low, waiting for a suitable time in which to make my final attempt to penetrate this mystery.

"I knew that for the adventure I was now contemplating considerable courage was required. But I did not hesitate. The time had come for me to show my mettle. In the few communications I was enabled to hold with my superiors I told them of my progress and arranged with them my plan of work. As we all agreed that I was about to encounter no common villainy, these plans naturally partook of finesse, as you will see if you will follow my narrative to the end.

"Early in the evening of a cool November night I sallied forth into the streets, dressed in the habiliments and wearing the guise of the wealthy old gentleman whose secret guest I had been for the last few days. As he was old and portly, and I young and spare, this disguise had cost me no little thought and labor. But assisted as I was by the darkness, I had but little fear of betraying myself to any chance spy who might be upon the watch, especially as Mr. L—— had a peculiar walk, which, in my short stay with him, I had learned to imitate perfectly. In the lapel of my overcoat I had tied a tag of blue ribbon, and, though for all I knew this was a signal devoting me to a secret and mysterious death, I walked along in a buoyant condition of mind, attributable, no doubt, to the excitement of the venture and to my desire to test my powers, even at the risk of my life.

"It was nine o'clock when I reached South Street. It was no new region to me, nor was I ignorant of the specified drinking den on the dock to which I had been directed. I remembered it as a bright spot in a mass of ship-prows and bow-rigging, and was possessed, besides, of a vague consciousness that there was something odd in connection with it which had aroused my curiosity sufficiently in the past for me to have once formed the resolution of seeing it again under circumstances which would allow me to give, it some attention. But I never thought that the circumstances would involve my own life, impossible as it is for a detective to reckon upon the future or to foresee the events into which he will be hurried by the next crime which may be reported at police headquarters.

"There were but few persons in the street when I crossed to The Heart's Delight,—so named from the heart-shaped opening in the framework of the door, through which shone a light, inviting enough to one chilled by the keen November air and oppressed by the desolate appearance of the almost deserted street. But amongst those persons I thought I recognized more than one familiar form, and felt reassured as to the watch which had been set upon the house. The night was dark and the river especially so, but in the gloomy space beyond the dock I detected a shadow blacker than the rest, which I took for the police-boat they had promised to have in readiness in case I needed rescue from the water-side. Otherwise the surroundings were as usual, and saving the gruff singing of some drunken sailor coming from a narrow side street near by, no sound disturbed the somewhat lugubrious silence of this weird and forsaken spot.

"Pausing an instant before entering, I glanced up at the building, which was about three stories high, and endeavored to see what there was about it which had once arrested my attention, and came to the conclusion that it was its exceptional situation on the dock, and the ghostly effect of the hoisting-beam projecting from the upper story like a gibbet. And yet this beam was common to many a warehouse in the vicinity, though in none of them were there any such signs of life as proceeded from the curious mixture of sail loft, boat shop and drinking saloon, now before me. Could it be that the ban of criminality was upon the house, and that I had been conscious of this without being able to realize the cause of my interest?

"Not stopping to solve my sensations further, I tried the door, and, finding it yield easily to my touch, turned the knob and entered. For a moment I was blinded by the smoky glare of the heated atmosphere into which I stepped, but presently I was able to distinguish the vague outlines of an oyster bar in the distance, and the motionless figures of some half dozen men, whose movements had been arrested by my sudden entrance. For an instant this picture remained; then the drinking and card-playing were resumed, and I stood, as it were, alone on the sanded floor near the door. Improving the opportunity for a closer inspection of the place, I was struck by its picturesqueness. It had evidently been once used as a ship chandlery, and on the walls, which were but partly plastered, there still hung old bits of marlin, rusty rings and such other evidences of former traffic as did not interfere with the present more lucrative business.

"Below were the two bars, one at the right of the door, and the other at the lower end of the room near a window, through whose small, square panes I caught a glimpse of the colored lights of a couple of ferry boats, passing each other in midstream.

"At a table near me sat two men, grumbling at each other over a game of cards. They were large and powerful figures in the contracted space of this long and narrow room, and my heart gave a bound of joy as I recognized on them certain marks by which I was to know friend from foe in this possible den of thieves and murderers.

"Two sailors at the bar were bona fide habitués of the place, and so I judged to be the one or two other specimens of water-side character whose backs I could faintly discern in one of the dim corners. Meantime a man was approaching me.

"Let me see if I can describe him. He was about thirty, and had the complexion and figure of a consumptive, but his eye shone with the yellow glare of a beast of prey, and in the cadaverous hollows of his ashen cheeks and amid the lines about his thin drawn lips there lay for all his conciliatory smile, an expression so cold and yet so ferocious that I spotted him at once as the man to whose genius we were indebted for the new scheme of murder which I was jeopardizing my life to understand. But I allowed none of the repugnance with which he inspired me to appear in my manner, and, greeting him with half a nod, waited for him to speak. His voice had that smooth quality which betrays the hypocrite.

"'Has the gentleman an appointment here?' he asked, letting his glance fall for the merest instant on the lapel of my coat.

"I returned a decided affirmative. Or rather, I went on, with a meaning look he evidently comprehended, 'my son has, and I have made up my mind to know just what deviltry he is up to these days. You see I can make it worth your while to give me the opportunity.'

"'O, I see,' he assented with a glance at the pocketbook I had just drawn out. 'You want a private room from which you can watch the young scapegrace. I understand, I understand. But the private rooms are above. Gentlemen are not comfortable here.'

"'I should say not,' I murmured, and drew from the pocketbook a bill which I slid quietly into his hand. 'Now take me where I shall be safe,' I suggested, 'and yet in full sight of the room where the young gentlemen play. I wish to catch him at his tricks. Afterwards——'

"'All will be well,' he finished smoothly, with another glance at my blue ribbon. 'You see I do not ask you the young gentleman's name. I take your money and leave all the rest to you. Only don't make a scandal, I pray, for my house has the name of being quiet.'

"'Yes,' thought I, 'too quiet!' and for an instant felt my spirits fail me. But it was only for an instant. I had friends about me and a pistol at half cock in the pocket of my overcoat. Why should I fear any surprise, prepared as I was for every emergency?

"'I will show you up in a moment,' said he; and left me to put up a heavy board-shutter over the window opening on the river. Was this a signal or a precaution? I glanced towards my two friends playing cards, took another note of their broad shoulders and brawny arms, and prepared to follow my host, who now stood bowing at the other end of the room, before a covered staircase which was manifestly the sole means of reaching the floor above.

"The staircase was quite a feature in the room. It ran from back to front, and was boarded all the way up to the ceiling. On these boards hung a few useless bits of chain, wire and knotted ends of tarred ropes, which swung to and fro as the sharp November blast struck the building, giving out a weird and strangely muffled sound. Why did this sound, so easily to be accounted for, ring in my ears like a note of warning? I understand now, but I did not then, full of expectation as I was for developments out of the ordinary.

"Crossing the room, I entered upon the staircase, in the wake of my companion. Though the two men at cards did not look up as I passed them, I noticed that they were alert and ready for any signal I might choose to give them. But I was not ready to give one yet. I must see danger before I summoned help, and there was no token of danger yet.

"When we were about half-way up the stairs the faint light which had illuminated us from below suddenly vanished, and we found ourselves in total darkness. The door at the foot had been closed by a careful hand, and I felt, rather than heard, the stealthy pushing of a bolt across it.

"My first impulse was to forsake my guide and rush back, but I subdued the unworthy impulse and stood quite still, while my companion exclaiming, 'Damn that fellow! What does he mean by shutting the door before we're half-way up!' struck a match and lit a gas jet in the room above, which poured a flood of light upon the staircase. Drawing my hand from the pocket in which I had put my revolver, I hastened after him into the small landing at the top of the stairs. An open door was before me, in which he stood bowing, with the half-burnt match in his hand. 'This is the place, sir,' he announced, motioning me in.

"I entered and he remained by the door, while I passed quickly about the room, which was bare of every article of furniture save a solitary table and chair. There was not even a window in it, with the exception of one small light situated so high up in the corner made by the jutting-up staircase that I wondered at its use, and was only relieved of extreme apprehension at the prison-like appearance of the place by the gleam of light which came through this dusty pane, showing that I was not entirely removed from the presence of my foes if I was from that of my friends.

"'Ah, you have spied the window,' remarked my host, advancing toward me with a countenance he vainly endeavored to make reassuring and friendly. 'That is your post of observation, sir,' he whispered, with a great show of mystery. 'By mounting on the table you can peer into the room where my young friends sit securely at play.'

"As it was not part of my scheme to show any special mistrust, I merely smiled a little grimly, and cast a glance at the table on which stood a bottle of brandy and one glass.

"'Very good brandy,' he whispered, 'Not such stuff as we give those fellows down-stairs.'

"I shrugged my shoulders and he slowly backed towards the door.

"'The young men you bid me watch are very quiet,' I suggested, with a careless wave of my hand towards the room he had mentioned.

"'Oh, there is no one there yet. They begin to straggle in about ten o'clock.'

"'Ah,' was my quiet rejoinder, 'I am likely, then, to have use for your brandy.'

"He smiled again and made a swift motion towards the door.

"'If you want anything,' said he, 'just step to the foot of the staircase and let me know. The whole establishment is at your service.' And with one final grin that remains in my mind as the most threatening and diabolical I have ever witnessed, he laid his hand on the knob of the door and slid quickly out.

"It was done with such an air of final farewell, that I felt my apprehensions take a positive form. Rushing towards the door through which he had just vanished, I listened and heard, as I thought, his stealthy feet descend the stair. But when I sought to follow, I found myself for the second time overwhelmed by darkness. The gas jet, which had hitherto burned with great brightness in the small room, had been turned off from below, and beyond the faint glimmer which found its way through the small window of which I have spoken, not a ray of light now disturbed the heavy gloom of this gruesome apartment.

"I had thought of every contingency but this, and for a few minutes my spirits were dashed. But I soon recovered some remnants of self-possession, and began feeling for the knob I could no longer see. Finding it after a few futile attempts, I was relieved to discover that this door at least was not locked; and, opening it with a careful hand, I listened intently, but could hear nothing save the smothered sound of men talking in the room below.

"Should I signal for my companions? No, for the secret was not yet mine as to how men passed from this room into the watery grave which was the evident goal for all wearers of the blue ribbon.

"Stepping back into the middle of the room, I carefully pondered my situation, but could get no further than the fact that I was somehow, and in some way, in mortal peril. Would it come in the form of a bullet, or a deadly thrust from an unseen knife? I did not think so. For, to say nothing of the darkness, there was one reassuring fact which recurred constantly to my mind in connection with the murders I was endeavoring to trace to this den of iniquity.

"None of the gentlemen who had been found drowned had shown any marks of violence on their bodies, so it was not attack I was to fear, but some mysterious, underhanded treachery which would rob me of consciousness and make the precipitation of my body into the water both safe and easy. Perhaps it was in the bottle of brandy that the peril lay; perhaps—but why speculate further! I would watch till midnight and then, if nothing happened, signal my companions to raid the house.

"Meantime a peep into the next room might help me towards solving the mystery. Setting the bottle and glass aside, I dragged the table across the floor, placed it under the lighted window, mounted, and was about to peer through, when the light in that apartment was put out also. Angry and overwhelmed, I leapt down, and, stretching out my hands till they touched the wainscoting, I followed the wall around till I came to the knob of the door, which I frantically clutched. But I did not turn it immediately, I was too anxious to catch these villains at work. Would I be conscious of the harm they meditated against me, or would I imperceptibly yield to some influence of which I was not yet conscious, and drop to the floor before I could draw my revolver or put to my mouth the whistle upon which I de-pended for assistance and safety? It was hard to tell, but I determined to cling to my first intention a little longer, and so stood waiting and counting the minutes, while wondering if the captain of the police boat was not getting impatient, and whether I had not more to fear from the anxiety of my friends than the cupidity of my foes.

"You see I had anticipated communicating with the men in this boat by certain signals and tokens which had been arranged between us. But the lack of windows in the room had made all such arrangements futile, so I knew as little of their actions as they of my sufferings; all of which did not tend to add to the cheerfulness of my position.

"I, however, held out for a half-hour, listening, waiting and watching in a darkness which, like that of Egypt, could be felt, and when the suspense grew intolerable I struck a match and let its blue flame flicker for a moment over the face of my watch. But the matches soon gave out and with them my patience, if not my courage, and I determined to end the suspense by knocking at the door beneath.

"This resolution taken, I pulled open the door before me and stepped out. Though I could see nothing, I remembered the narrow landing at the top of the stairs, and, stretching out my arms, I felt for the boarding on either hand, guilding myself by it, and began to descend, when something rising, as it were, out of the cavernous darkness before me made me halt and draw back in mingled dread and horror.

"But the impression, strong as it was, was only momentary, and, resolved to be done with the matter, I precipitated myself downward, when suddenly, at about the middle of the staircase, my feet slipped and I slid forward, plunging and reaching out with hands whose frenzied grasp found nothing to cling to, down a steep inclined plane—or what to my bewildered senses appeared such,—till I struck a yielding surface and passed with one sickening plunge into the icy waters of the river which in another moment had closed dark and benumbing above my head.

"It was all so rapid I did not think of uttering a cry. But happily for me the splash I made told the story, and I was rescued before I could sink a second time.

"It was a full half hour before I had sufficiently recovered from the shock to relate my story. But when once I had made it known, you can imagine the gusto with which the police prepared to enter the house and confound the obliging host with a sight of my dripping garments and accusing face. And indeed in all my professional experience I have never beheld a more sudden merging of the bully into a coward than was to be seen in this slick villain's face, when I was suddenly pulled from the crowd and placed before him, with the old man's wig gone from my head, and the tag of blue ribbon still clinging to my wet coat.

"His game was up, and he saw it; and Ebenezer Gryce's career had begun.

"Like all destructive things the device by which I had been run into the river was simple enough when understood. In the first place it had been constructed to serve the purpose of a stairway and chute. The latter was in plain sight when it was used by the sailmakers to run the finished sails into the waiting yawls below. At the time of my adventure, and for some time before, the possibilities of the place had been discovered by mine host, who had ingeniously put a partition up the entire stairway, dividing the steps from the smooth runway. At the upper part of the runway he had built a few steps, wherewith to lure the unwary far enough down to insure a fatal descent. To make sure of his game he had likewise ceiled the upper room all around, including the enclosure of the stairs. The door to the chute and the door to the stairs were side by side, and being made of the same boards as the wainscoting, were scarcely visible when closed, while the single knob that was used, being transferable from one to the other, naturally gave the impression that there was but one door. When this adroit villain called my attention to the little window around the corner, he no doubt removed the knob from the stairs' door and quickly placed it in the one opening upon the chute. Another door, connecting the two similar landings without, explains how he got from the chute staircase into which he passed, on leaving me, to the one communicating with the room below.

"The mystery was solved, and my footing on the force secured; but to this day—and I am an old man now—I have not forgotten the horror of the moment when my feet slipped from under me, and I felt myself sliding downward, without hope of rescue, into a pit of heaving waters, where so many men of conspicuous virtue had already ended their valuable lives.

"Myriad thoughts flashed through my brain in that brief interval, and among them the whole method of operating this death-trap, together with every detail of evidence that would secure the conviction of the entire gang."

End of the book.